To _____

From _____

Other giftbooks by Helen Exley:
Daughters ...   For My Father
Sisters ...   Best of Father Quotations
Brothers ...   For Mother – A Gift of Love

Published simultaneously in 1997 by Exley Publications in Great Britain, and
Exley Giftbooks in the USA.
Copyright © Helen Exley 1997

The moral right of Helen Exley has been asserted.

12 11 10 9 8 7 6 5 4 3 2

Border illustrations by Juliette Clarke
Edited and pictures selected by Helen Exley

ISBN 1-85015-791-X

Picture research by Image Select, London.
Typeset by Delta, Watford.
Printed and bound in China

Exley Publications Ltd, 16 Chalk Hill, Watford, Herts. WD1 4BN.
Exley Giftbooks, 232 Madison Avenue, Suite 1206, NY 10016, USA.

DADS...

A HELEN EXLEY GIFTBOOK

NEW YORK • WATFORD, UK

A father is a very ordinary man who must take on the most important job in the world.

A father is a man who has relinquished his freedom. Gladly.

A father is a man who places his children above all other achievements.

A father is the man who makes a good life for his children, protects them, guides them, standing by them in times of trouble.

A father is someone overwhelmed to find he is so loved and so needed.

PAM BROWN, b.1928

... MY DAD IS MY HERO. Not a statue in the park, not just another pretty face without blemishes, not just a black bow tie and black patent leather shoes, always going away. I'm never free of a problem nor do
I truly experience a joy until we share it. I need him to know when I'm hurting. I need him to know when I'm happy. I need him to know, to hear me, and in that I am no different from every daughter and, I suppose, son.

NANCY SINATRA, b.1940,
FROM "FRANK SINATRA: MY FATHER"

Dad, you are our king – tall and strong and wise
and full of laughter. Never dismiss your life as
commonplace.

PAM BROWN, b.1928

To a young boy, the father is a giant from whose
shoulders you can see forever.

PERRY GARFINKEL

Father: Someone we can look up to no matter
how tall we get.

ANONYMOUS

A new father is a man dizzy with almost disbelieving joy.

PAM BROWN, b.1928

Suddenly, a most ordinary man becomes special.

HELEN THOMSON, b.1943

From Hugh J. O'Neill there came a pulse that felt, to his son, like a promise. There would be much to learn in this life. There would be stories to hear. Life would offer a guy all he could handle.

HUGH O'NEILL

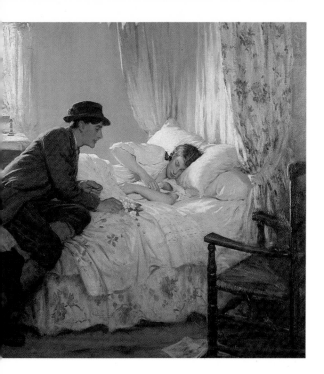

I could not point to any need in childhood as strong as that for a father's protection.

SIGMUND FREUD (1856-1939)

Every day of my life has been a gift from him. His lap had been my refuge from lightning and thunder. His arms had sheltered me from teenage heartbreak. His wisdom and understanding had sustained me as an adult.

NELLIE PIKE RANDALL

A father is the hands that hold you safe.

JANE SWAN, b.1943

AND THEN THERE IS LOVE

What I have learned in the process of raising
(four) daughters – and perhaps it applies to oth
human affairs as well – is that there is no single
answer, no magic formula, no rigid set of
guidelines, no simple blueprint, no book of eas
instructions, no sure way of side-stepping
difficulties, no easy way out. There is love.

GEORGE LEONARD

Any man can become a father. It takes love to
become a dad.

MARION C. GARRETTY, b.1917

used to think only of the body parts involved in becoming a dad. The body parts needed for conceiving Isaac, lifting Isaac, throwing a ball to Isaac, wrestling with Isaac.

But that's not right, of course.

These body parts are mere bystanders to love. I finally have accepted the idea, after years of merely realizing it, that if I had never gotten well physically, it still would have been possible for me to become Isaac's father in every way that mattered. My heart has to perform well.

That's all that matters.

ART KLEIN, FROM *"DAD AND SON"*

Don't take up a man's time talking about the smartness of your children; he wants to talk to you about the smartness of his.

E.W. HOWE

There must be such a thing as a child with average ability, but you can't find a parent who will admit that it is his child.... Start a program for gifted children, and every parent demands that his child is enrolled.

THOMAS D. BAILEY,
FROM *"WALL STREET JOURNAL"*, DECEMBER 17, 1962

Fathers are what give daughters away to other men who aren't nearly good enough...
so they can have grandchildren that are smarter than anybody's.

PAUL HARVEY

A father is a banker provided by nature.

FRENCH PROVERB

If a man smiles at home somebody is sure to ask him for money.

WILLIAM FEATHER

A father is someone who doesn't only pay for his *own* mistakes – he usually ends up paying for his children's as well.

MIKE KNOWLES

Any father could teach any business guru a thing or two.

JENNY DE VRIES

Not every year, of course, do I get Old Spice or underwear. Many times a few of my kids are away from home on this special day, but they always remember to call me collect, thus allowing the operator to join in the Father's Day wishes too.

BILL COSBY, b.1937, FROM *"FATHERHOOD"*

I WATCHED A SMALL MAN WITH THICK

CALLUSES ON BOTH HANDS WORK FIFTEEN

AND SIXTEEN HOURS A DAY. I SAW HIM ONCE

LITERALLY BLEED FROM THE BOTTOMS OF HIS

FEET, A MAN WHO CAME HERE UNEDUCATED,

ALONE, UNABLE TO SPEAK THE LANGUAGE, WHO

TAUGHT ME ALL I NEEDED TO KNOW ABOUT

FAITH AND HARD WORK BY THE SIMPLE

ELOQUENCE OF HIS EXAMPLE.

MARIO CUOMO

A FATHER IS...

... a man who drops everything
and comes running at the sound of a
thump or a wail.

... the executive who nods off at conferences
having walked the teething baby all
night long.

... the man who stops to exchange kisses
with his baby half way down the
supermarket aisle.

... the man who has finger paintings pinned
up in the office.

... the man who helps you clear the place up just before Mother is due back.

... the man who embarrasses you by applauding you too loudly.

... the sound of the car, the tread of footsteps on the path, the click of the key in the lock – the arms spread out to catch you.

... the man who manages to look thrilled to bits when you give him socks for his birthday – again.

PAM BROWN, b.1928

The great man is he who does not lose his child's heart.

MENCIUS

My love for my father has never been touched or approached by any other love. I hold him in my heart of hearts as a man apart from all other men, as one apart from all other beings.

MAMIE DICKENS (1836-1896),
FROM *"MY FATHER AS I RECALL HIM"*

Who, pyjama clad and bleary-eyed, carried me all about the house to soothe my wailing to a whimper – and so at last to sleep?

Who made up mumps stories and chicken pox stories and stories to suit a broken leg?

Who cuddled me up when the wind roared and the rain hammered and the thunder rolled and the lightning filled the sky?

Who has always stood between me and fear?

My Dad.

PAM BROWN, b.1928

Dad has to instantly absorb info on car seats, croup, origami, and oatmeal, stuff a man without kids simply does not have to master. Dad has to know how to get a tiny stretchy sock on a humid kid foot, how to get a giant frayed shoelace through a teensy little shoelace hole, and how to repair a doll's earring.

HUGH O'NEILL, FROM *"A MAN CALLED DADDY"*

Parents were invented to make children happy
by giving them something to ignore.

OGDEN NASH (1902-1971)

What's the difference between a doctor
and a dad?
Well, when a doctor gives you some advice you
usually accept it.

MIKE KNOWLES

There comes a time when you have to face the fact
that Dad has forgotten how to do algebra.

SAM BROWN, b.1928

If you must hold yourself up to your children,
hold yourself up as an object lesson and not as
an example.

GEORGE BERNARD SHAW (1856-1950)

SO, NOTHING MUCH CHANGES!

By the time a man realizes that his father was usually right, he has a child who thinks he's usually wrong.

DR. LAURENCE J. PETER

Society moves by some degree of parricide, by which children, on the whole, kill, if not their fathers, at least the beliefs of their fathers and arrive at new beliefs. That is what progress is.

SIR ISAIAH BERLIN, b.1912

Children have never been very good at listening to their elders, but they have never failed to imitate them.

JAMES BALDWIN (1924-1987),
FROM *"NOBODY KNOWS MY NAME"*

The children despise their parents until the age of forty, when they suddenly become just like them — thus preserving the system.

QUENTIN CREWE

It is difficult to say when the thing started, but little by little the American Father has become established on the television screen as Nature's last work in saps, boobs, and total losses, the man with two left feet who can't move in any direction without falling over himself. Picture a rather IQ-less village idiot and you will have the idea. Father, as he appears in what is known in television circles as a heart-warming domestic comedy, is a bohunkus who could walk straight into any establishment for the feeble-minded and no questions asked.

P.G. WODEHOUSE (1881-1975)

It never occurs to a boy that he will some day be as dumb as his father.

DR. LAURENCE J. PETER

I had heard all those things about fatherhood, how great it is. But it's greater than I'd ever expected – I had no idea Quinton would steal my heart the way he has. From the minute I laid eyes on him, I knew nobody could ever wrestle him away from me.

BURT REYNOLDS, b. 1936

Nothing I've ever done has given me more joys and rewards than being a father to my children.

BILL COSBY, b.1937

I'm a father. It's what I've always wanted to be. It's what I almost always love doing. It is the only thing in my life that day in and out makes me feel like a good man. A real man.

ART KLEIN, FROM *"DAD AND SON"*

What gift has providence bestowed on man that is so dear to him as his children?

CICERO (106-43 B.C.)

A father is a man whose days are illuminated by his childrens' smiles.

PAM BROWN, b.1928

A baby can teach the clumsiest of men infinite gentleness.

MARION C. GARRETTY, b.1917

A father scurries around fixing baby gates and bannisters, safety locks and cat proof doors. He wants above all else to keep his new life, this utterly vulnerable creature, from all harm.

CHARLOTTE GRAY, b.1928

"TWO SMALL VOICES IN MY SOUL"

Since I have been a father, the pendulum of my life swings through a wider arc. Before Josh and Rebecca, I rarely whispered and I rarely yelled. Now I do both all the time. Before Josh and Rebecca, I merely strode through the world like a man. Now I crawl, hunker, scramble, hop on one foot, often see the world from my hands and knees. Before Josh and Rebecca, I knew nothing about waterslides. Now I hold several American records

over-thirty-five division. Before Josh and
Rebecca, I heard only the sound of my own voice.
Now I sometimes hear the principal, asking to see
me at my "earliest possible convenience." Now I
always carry two small voices in my soul. Before
Josh and Rebecca, the world was plain. Now it's
fancy, full of portents and omens, comic books and
ant farms, solemnity and awe.

HUGH O'NEILL, FROM *"A MAN CALLED DADDY"*

LITTLE MONSTERS! MINI DICTATORS!

A child's thumb is minuscule – but its father is firmly under it.

MAYA V. PATEL, b.1928

...ad has long and earnest conversations with
...s baby daughter. He tells her she is noisy,
...disciplined and manipulative – and
...e will be sent back if she doesn't pull herself
...gether.
...d the baby smiles complacently.
...e has him exactly where she wants him.

...M BROWN, b.1928

...rents are not quite interested in justice, they
...e interested in quiet.

...LL COSBY, b.1937

...thers should be neither seen nor heard. That
...the only proper basis for family life.

...CAR WILDE (1856 – 1900)

Changed for life

*B*ecoming a father changes everything. And I do mean everything: the way you speak, the way you work, sleep, drive, eat, dress, think. It even changes what you sing. Fatherhood changes your posture, your sex life, your hairstyle, your feelings about money, politics, God, about your past, and about the planet's future. Children change the ground you walk on.

HUGH O'NEILL, FROM "A MAN CALLED DADDY"

*N*othing changes a guy's life more drastically than fatherhood. One day, you're cruising down life's fast lane with the top down, wind in your hair and "Born to Be Wild" blaring on the stereo. The next thing you know, you're poking along near the right shoulder in your station wagon, singing silly songs about some old man who plays knickknack paddywhack on other people's knees....

JIM PARKER

HERE we were. Quite an odd couple. Shy with each other in ways; each other's intimate mind reader in other ways. An intimacy based more on memories of what we had meant to each other than on what we had said. At peace finally over who was dad. Each other's dad and son. Sharing the driving in Dad's car because it was more comfortable for him than sitting in my truck. I not minding in the least Dad's chauffeuring me around when I needed to stretch out on the backseat to ease my muscles. Both of us unabashedly happy in the way boys are to be with a favorite playmate.

ART KLEIN, FROM *"DAD AND SON"*

I suppose that the single most important factor in my upbringing [was] a sense of security and a sense of confidence which my father gave to all his children, and even if I said something foolish, he gave it as much weight as though it were the most wonderful insight.

BENAZIR BHUTTO

There have been many times when I thought other people might be better singers or better musicians or prettier than me, but then I would hear Daddy's voice telling me to never say never, and I would find a way to squeeze an extra inch or two out of what God had given me.

BARBARA MANDRELL

Life doesn't come with an instruction book
— that's why we have fathers.

H. JACKSON BROWN

I talk and talk and talk, and I haven't
taught people in fifty years what my father
taught by example in one week.

MARIO CUOMO

The young man knows the rules, but the old
man knows the exceptions.

OLIVER WENDELL HOLMES (1809-1894)

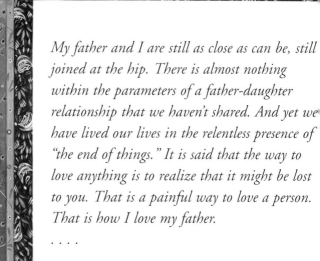

My father and I are still as close as can be, still joined at the hip. There is almost nothing within the parameters of a father-daughter relationship that we haven't shared. And yet we have lived our lives in the relentless presence of "the end of things." It is said that the way to love anything is to realize that it might be lost to you. That is a painful way to love a person. That is how I love my father.

. . . .

When he is gone, when it is "done and done," I won't have to watch his films or play his recordings to remember, I'll carry his blood in my veins, his life's music in my heart and see his immortal soul in the bright, loving eyes of my children.

NANCY SINATRA, b.1940,
FROM *"FRANK SINATRA: MY FATHER"*

It's a wonderful feeling when your father becomes not a god but a man to you – when he comes down from the mountain and you see he's this man with weaknesses. And you love him as this whole being, not as a figurehead.

ROBIN WILLIAMS

You worship him as a hero,
then despise him as a man.
Eventually you love him as a human being.

PAM BROWN, b.1928

MEMORIES

He invented humorous songs and ditties, and made up
stories about landmarks which we passed on car journeys
An ordinary house became the lair where a giant kept his
toothbrush; another was compulsorily purchased – in his
imagination only – as a store
for his books. He was also a brilliant mimic.
He could be kind. When, at 11, I knitted
a hat for him – it looked like an aborted tea cosy – he
wore it up to London on the train.

CRESSIDA CONNOLLY,
IN THE *"DAILY MAIL"*, 25TH MARCH 1995

I remember his hands holding me while, as a child, I learned to swim, firm but gentle hands keeping me safe. I remember those same hands guiding me, balancing me, and then letting go, as I tried to ride a two-wheeler. I remember lunches with him at drive-ins, oil painting with him on the back porch, baseball games, where he taught me the rules. And I remember the bear hug he gave me recently when I told him how *much I* love him. I could feel the vibration of the sigh in his chest against my cheek. "Oohh," he said, "I'd turn the world upside down for you."

NANCY SINATRA, b.1940,
FROM "FRANK SINATRA: MY FATHER"

Romance fails us and so do friendships, but the relationship of parent and child, less noisy than all others, remains indelible and indestructible, the strongest relationship on earth.

THEODOR REIK

Somewhere I remember drowsing in the crook of your arm, listening to reading – voice and tale and firelight blurring into one. So far. So long ago. Yet part of my mind and heart forever.

PAM BROWN, b.1928

The ordinary father

After all, the world depends upon the ordinary work of ordinary people, and foremost in these ranks we find the ordinary father. In fact he's so ordinary that few, if any, of us pay any attention to him or take note of his coming or going. Even to himself he scarcely takes credit for the place he fills in the world.

Yet, consider: Could the work of the world move on without this man? Could society exist without his ceaseless efforts?

No! The fathers of the world bear that part of the world's work that can be borne by no one else so well. They make of the fabric of society a cloth of gold and set the homes as gems thereon. They plan and work, succeed or fail as the world judges success or failure. They give of their strength and endurance, of their energy and ambition, of their dreams of happiness and their lessons of experience and we take them all as common offerings, failing to appraise them at a quota of their real value.

Let us now, in the rush of life, render love, reverence and justice to this man — the ordinary father.

MINNIE KEITH BAILEY,
QUOTED IN *"DEAR OLD FATHER"*, 1910

I took for granted all his kindly ways; I only knew I liked him best of all, and that the days with him were golden days. How often, when a man, I have wished when my father was behind my chair, that he would pass his hand over my hair, as he used to do when I was a boy.

FRANCIS DARWIN (ED.)
(1848-1925),
FROM *"LIFE AND LETTERS
OF CHARLES DARWIN"*

Acknowledgements: The publishers are grateful for permission to reproduce copyright material. Whilst every effort has been made to trace copyright holders, the publishers would be pleased to hear from any not here acknowledged. MINNIE KEITH BAILEY: Extract from "The Ordinary Father" in *Dear Old Father* published by The Goldsmith-Woolard Publishing Co, Wichita. 1910. ART KLEIN: Extracts from *Dad and Son*, © Art Klein 1996. Reprinted by permission of the author. HUGH O'NEILL: Extracts from *A Man Called Daddy*, © Hugh O'Neill 1996. Reprinted by permission of Rutledge Hill Press, Nashville. NANCY SINATRA: Extracts from *Frank Sinatra: My Father*, © Nancy Sinatra 1985. Reprinted by permission of the author.

Picture Credits: Exley Publications is very grateful to the following individuals and organisations for permission to reproduce their pictures: Superstock (SS), Archiv für Kunst (AKG), The Bridgeman Art Library (BAL), The Image Bank (TIB), Statens Konstmuseer